GÜERA

GÜERA

REBECCA GAYDOS

OMNIDAWN PUBLISHING
OAKLAND, CALIFORNIA
2016

Cover art © JW Collinge, courtesy of Santa Barbara Vintage Photos

Cover and interior typefaces: Minion Pro and Optima LT Std

Cover and interior design by Gillian Olivia Blythe Hamel

Offset printed in the United States
by Edwards Brothers Malloy, Ann Arbor, Michigan
On 55# Glatfelter B18 Antique
Acid Free Archival Quality Recycled Paper

Library of Congress Cataloging-in-Publication Data

Names: Gaydos, Rebecca, 1984- author.
  Title: Güera / Rebecca Gaydos.
  Description: Oakland, California : Omnidawn Publishing, 2016. | "This is the
  author's first book of poetry" -- Publisher's comment.
  Identifiers: LCCN 2016014891 | ISBN 9781632430243 (pbk. : alk. paper)
  Classification: LCC PS3607.A985728 A6 2016 | DDC 811/.6--dc23
  LC record available at https://lccn.loc.gov/2016014891

Published by Omnidawn Publishing, Oakland, California
www.omnidawn.com (510) 237-5472 (800) 792-4957
10 9 8 7 6 5 4 3 2 1
ISBN: 978-1-63243-024-3

CONTENTS

ARCTIC DREAM

My mother told me I should try to do some artwork so that I could get my own
money. When my husband told me to go to my mother to get a dollar to go to the
movies, she told me, You know how to draw, so do some artwork

autonomy's a long, long joke
imagine the Arctic and the cliché itself becomes intangible, snow-globish

the cliché itself came one day, it looked into the image of my image
it doubted my mobile ways

it whispered dirty things in my ear about Hostelling International
then it unwhispered those same things

art being the thing among things that is not itself a thing

I want to say to her,
            you're always open

about art because you made it
            tourist from the get-go

in a dream the emphasis is on

                              open
'she's open'
has no ring to it,
 no unsavory flavor,
 no quickening of the heart

then outside of the dream
there's the usual chorus,

            all the little sculptures   will go down south
            all the big sculptures   will get filmed

TINY'S

John Henry was a steel-driving man

Tiny, take this hammer.

After John Henry didn't wake up she got a hammer
at a women-owned tattoo collective in San Francisco

This is my third try at John Henry.

If I keep trying I'll make a joke about keep on keeping on—

I'll make it stupid, small, spent

I wrote you a letter and it went like this:

Tiny's is about John Henry. It's a John Henry poem.

Won't you name your baby Henry because you want to name it John Henry but are just a little shy to do it

Won't you name your baby

You won't name your baby Tiny's even though you might as well because Tiny's is about John Henry and you wish you named your baby John Henry not just plain Henry but you were shy

You call it Henry because you don't know that Tiny's is a John Henry poem so you might as well call your poem and your baby Tiny's

Why not call your whole property Tiny's?

If Tiny's is about John Henry, Tiny's is legendary and Tiny's is a good source.

So you should name your baby Tiny's and then you will say what you want to say.

Tiny's is about girls between the ages of 19 and 22.

So if you name your baby Henry you think it won't be named Tiny's later.

But you are stupid because Tiny's is about John Henry.

So if you name your baby Henry it is named Tiny's.

The way not to name your baby Tiny's is to not like the bodies of thin small women to haunt the bigger mean bodies. But the thin small bodies have little logical patterns. And they are bitchy of course. And if you sit next to one go ahead and put your arm on the shared space of the armrest because since they are so small they do not really need that space so you should just take it and call it Tiny's.

At Magoo's
John Henry taught me how to play Keno

'Tiny'
could sound tough
if you said,
"Don't fuck with Tiny."

No one sings about me.

I thought about a story and it went like this:

In my mind the party at my apartment was unauthorized, and when the girls wanted to play strip poker my boyfriend had no objection, one girl read aloud excerpts from her journal, another girl said she was really in the mood for a cock in her mouth, my boyfriend said "there's a lot of cocks in this room," I walked into my room and found a girl and a golden-retriever asleep on the bed,

then I summoned a biker-gang, I imagined myself playing pool and winning,

in retrospect I should have let the dumb bitch suck my boyfriend's cock because it would have meant less work for me

even though my fortune said,

Don't focus on an outcome
Set your house
Wait on the will of heaven

Their sharpie on my refrigerator, 'ugly bitch' they wrote, which I thought was implausible, in any case, it's dumbness that one fears, it's the whole body, or the mouth

He is going to hitchhike
Right through

Right through the Pacific Northwest
He wants to enter me from behind
On his birthday

I kept coming up
with alternatives,
maybe I'd go work on a WWOOF farm

Play this up—
I got into the bed of a truck to get a ride up the mountain. I want you to feel what I
look like when I'm being this way. The image gets big and goes back in, it goes to
the head.

A Ka-Bar is a special kind of knife
You can work your way through, you can skin it

You can get Guns & Ammo at the pizza shop
Even in Berkeley, California you can get a look at it in one pizza shop except it
closed down about two years ago.

What is he?

He's Catholic-atheist. He's white-Irish. He's pulling out of me.

Tiny is here with a Marine-issued knife. She's picking one out for you. She's
thumbing the catalogue. The first section is called Ka-Bar. The second section
is called hammer. The third section is called gun show.

He wasn't fully casual or fully wry. He just said the kitchen faucet likes to get
slapped around a little bit.

Tiny's got a knife that can get taken away from her. It's about turning. For me
I didn't try to do things the original way. I just got recursive enough.

Once a child playing in the dusk said to me & B., Look, I'm collecting seeds. Her
dad said, They don't need to know what you're doing. We were so into that.
Because the father was a real redneck. If I could map this moment onto my
own wardrobe, onto the drinks I order, and the moves I make. But instead it's
migrated into this knife business. Ka-Bar this, Ka-Bar that.

When I walked into it
It was at the exact moment that a man said his fantasy was to fuck a petite blond
girl on roller skates. I wasn't blond or on roller skates but everyone was in hysterics,
a serendipitous entrance.

B. never mentioned John Henry was black

Something about me
in the throes of explanation.

It's *wrong* to say—
        the story was all along
        all along I was being loved and desired
        all along I was in the claws of power
        coupling with retribution
        on the underside

I heard about folk songs.

Here's a John Henry story. There was a girl named Tiny who didn't need tattoos because her body was perfect. In Mexico she met a girl named Paulina who told her about names that women use to call their cleaning ladies. Tiny drank whiskey and smoked and looked really good naked.

A little north of downtown Oakland outside the Adams Point Whole Foods
my friend told me his favorite race is white girls with ass

Thinking twice,
Puts you with something plain.

But to get back to John Henry, let me be frank—

> My sister complained about the psychic she went to. Why did she spend
> $50 to have a woman chain smoking in penguin pajama pants tell her that
> her crown chakra is blocked?

> But even if you go to a psychic, this is still America, so you shouldn't
> expect anyone to be like this or that. You shouldn't expect anything per se
> based on a profession. You shouldn't think this person is going to look like
> a magical person with powers. You shouldn't say your favorite race is
> white girls with ass. But all along I thought my better half looked like John
> Henry but I imagined that John Henry looked like Jesse James.

Present me to myself through a big disguise

It looked like a piece of cherry pie

Graffitied on the side of the road, by the vines

Ask me, do I know what cherry pie meant

Musically,

to whom?

Once a man stood in the vines naked with a white sock on his penis and this was on 50th Avenue.

When I stood there I looked
at the vines, at the cherry pie, at that exhibitionist in his white sock. It's all incidental that this happened here. It's not like he said, I'm going to stand in the vines with a white sock on my penis because there is a piece of cherry pie painted on the concrete behind the vines on 50th Avenue.

I'm coming home

Staring at the pie painting

I can't tell what it stands for because I didn't already know and I'm no good at looking at things.

I've gone off of music.

I got a lot of you transmitted.

I'm afraid of disability.

Of not having legs.

Of tasting great.

You jump into legends.

But I'm curving back around.

I hand it in that way.

It's 6PM.

Call it sundown.

Who gets into John Henry

Who tells it like they know

I sent an email to my friend saying, sure, I'll give you your dress back, but I've been around
the block in it.

I can't possibly make this about myself.

Tiny all the way through.

GÜERA

Poor Mexico, so far from God, so close to the United States

GÜERA

pobre México, tan lejos de Dios y tan cerca de los Estados Unidos

tú eres   *güera*
cuando caminas en la calle, ellos dicen   *güera*

nobody could translate güera into white girl
not straight up   but by a twist in your heart
maybe they could

remark is obvious,
remark's a side helping,

a loosely pejorative
topographical joust

it's appearance's sound,

it's that look's talk
makes you look
            straight ahead

you rig up your walk on

I've always had nicknames,
address has form like none other

(among ourselves
 we're saying 'lady'
with lady you put yourself close

if you're gonna give it over,
give over your colloquial heart,
admit the off-handedness,
the shrug that passes through, *lady*)

since güera is comparative, adjectival, always interpolating, —it specifies
something other than nationality—it's a wide-mouthed way to talk about look,
to sound off in the street, to address, to flag, to get up on what's obvious, what
appears here.

the obvious stopped being obvious
it slipped
left me wet

THE LAND BEFORE TIME

I was born naturally
in the 1980s in a birth center in Goleta, CA   .

naturally is what happens if your mom doesn't have an epidural

but what's the point of all these riddles

Paco's history lesson had this joke—
A name includes a nahual
A nahual is whichever animal first crosses the baby's path
So Juan ended up Juan Bicicleta

MEZCALITA

mezcalita, mezcalita
cookie cut my güera way

the curious structure of a stereotype
with my braids I looked

like Sabrina the teenage witch

when we touch each other this late in the game
it's called tourism

MAZUNTE

(museo de la tortuga)

Tortuga, glass bound like he is—

The best anthropomorphic moment of my life was watching the tortuga hump
the pole in the aquarium.

Graceful, yes. the patterns
on his skin—
there were güeros too
the albino eye blinks pink

at least sentience has a look
there's a style to these encounters

baby, please don't be so stuck on the untranslatable elements of nonhuman life
there's a look to things
the stinky aquarium's got a look
the tortuga eye has got a look

BAÑO TURCO

After the screening, Eveli from Veracruz approached me. We had coffee and chocolate cake. Talked about our boyfriends. Walked home in a downpour.

Tell the tourist trinket
from the luscious, museum-quality
reproductions from the real
treasures of tomb 7?

Tell the fortified ruins
from the real deal ruins

Today a man gave me a ride on his motorcycle. He found me walking in Xochimilco near the aqueducts and offered me a ride to the centro. It was a chance encounter and though it ought to have carried the weight of potential sexual disaster, it was neutral, a blank shot. When I smiled I was checking ride-on-the-back-of-a-motorcycle off my life list.

On the other hand, Eveli from Veracruz was more complicated. She was offering and asking at the same time. She had combinatorial prowess.

Look's no layer
not a veil hanging down
or flung back

appearance doesn't put me in the mood
for topography

nothing to traverse, nothing to cast off

THE IMAGE OF THE FLAMING

the image of the flaming heart
looks better in strong colors

countries coagulate into a hemisphere

the conversational level

Gaby asks me to translate words
then she doubts my translations

strange skeletons—
in the states it's bobble heads
from time to time

here it's the life of the diorama
the stand alone, the ready scene

handy heart, crafty like that
I want to reproduce with you

Los Angeles is understandable
one way or another

MI VIDA, MI CIELO

in identity's interstices
nobody gives 2 shits about my or your endorsement
the will's curvaceous

a certain blue in the sky
is more recognizable than certain others

talking the talk
there's *mi vida, mi cielo*, there's baby

I am left vague with my lets, wills, gets, & dos

the 4th of July party
was 50% Mexican, 50% "American"
(I tried to be cool by saying I had forgotten it was the 4th & my friend
tried to be cool by saying she had forgotten)
(this resulted in a communist joke

                    which has lost the "ring of truth"
                    it's a joke on time itself, getting late)

the sky is sometimes specific

Clapton's Cocaine sounds
the same everywhere

I'm popular like top 20, like tradition

a little bit married, a little bit pregnant
I don't miss my bf unless I hear old country

if opacity's sexy,
gradation's the ball breaker

ROMANCE LANGUAGE PART I

I got vague

I was Shelly selling s. by the s.

saying stuff,

hand it over
fill it in
add some
fuck me good
give me a hand
put a lot of effort
to be very mad
it pains me
to madden
to miss

to be disaffected's nothing new

reciprocation went blank
went static went snow

reciprocation mustered itself

reciprocation plays the informal market

it occurs in the looks of it

ROMANCE LANGUAGE PART II

Look's no cipher for desire

it is not a backhand deal

desire was a ways off
a puffy heirloom
        bent on elegiac ways

GÜERA II: THE FEDERAL DISTRICT

Commercial heart, somebody's turf.

Myself looking at myself in the green field inside the big state.

There were pockets of men wandering about, tinkering with motorcycles.

I encourage people to be happy about their adventures

but the account of the center is what I got dumb giving,

because it is self-explanatory and I was part of the explaining self

Kerouac in D.F.—but why have a straw man?

If I could show you that colloquial talk is poetic, my dream would be to show you this without an attitude.

Even if I could give a critique, I would not,

instead: my own image, the basic transaction

buey = "poner los cuernos"
horns, to be cheated on (this back in the 50s & 60s
which eventually became güey, or on the internet wey or just we

in prison, when speaking w/ inmates no one uses 'güey' b/c of the original meaning
(everyone in prison assuming that their lady is w/ someone else now)...instead,
they use carnal...blood brother

in exchange for all this, I told him the word 'beaver' has an obscene meaning

his hands are little-girl sized

in my country I'm a small woman but now I'm not in my country

the plan was to make camisetas
on the front saying, I HATE GRINGOS
on the back saying,
I LOVE GRINGAS

Another idea was to put the words
PINK CHEESE
GREEN GO

spiritual exercises—

1. imagine a blond lady with who

2. you have the mentality of what? he talks of oreos and coconuts. he says American women don't do anything unless they want to. on the other hand, he thought maybe when they show their breasts in the street (mardi gras? spring break?) they don't want to. To want to? It raises the question, *what?*

And yes, I too was pissed about art.

Appearance is what something is to something else.

Downstairs two women have been conversing, having coffee, over a manuscript. It's thick and they handle it pushing it back into the manila envelope or back into a plastic baggie, a plastic covering.

Last night there was a joke about minimalism. Real minimalism is not ecological because you have these weird lights that you put under your walls and leave running all the time so your walls will be floating

This whole huge distinction between his cousin who would search for photographs of Kurt Cobain and buy clothing accordingly versus in his case *just happening* to wear the same shoes and jeans as Cobain. Still, maybe this is the what. In either case. I'm not the only person.

My nation is flocking.

I don't want to make everything a hotbed for art, or everything like me. That's what the countries were for. And yet the mystique of the popular is still meaning something to my gotten heart. Since I'm from California I am often elongating my vowels. I wouldn't trade my pueblo for the clearest English, not for even half a jet-setting soul. My ancestors fought in the American Revolution so technically speaking I could be a DAR.

The heart is a stupid heart, it was put here by the countries. One girl was so drunk she was carried off with pee in her pants. Since my pants were black my pee would be white. But somehow the joke came off racial.

he says the reason he's always liked white women has nothing to do with colonialism,
rather, it's anti-oedipal. Freud, the nation-state, these types of things
are part of the explanation

here to make an exchange

look at me

but it meant something to me, whatever the time,

the templo mayor is an edge of the zócalo
outside the people dressed up in feathers,

a regular image
in the tourist heart, the local heart

this is my derivation, this is the longest look I can give you

if I were to show my own long look, the story of the story we all told
I'd watch an 18-year-old blond girl spread out on the hood of what kind of car in Texas,
a place I've never been to,

There's a part that traces the nation back to brown women getting fucked by white men. And one page has a woman holding a baby. And then another page asks why the Indian men didn't fuck the white women. And the answer given is that there weren't any. I was given this book on my birthday. Well actually a few days later because on my actual birthday he didn't have a gift for me. We walked around the park and I said all the things that the vendors sell look like crap.

Another day we went to the Adidas store in La Condesa, because he wanted to. He asked how much the Mexico jersey was and the guy that worked there told him. And after they lose to Argentina? The guy snapped, *The same*, before correcting himself, *What do you mean lose?* I looked at another man in the store and we both started giggling.

the most basic is within one's expanded hemisphere

in terms of California it's hard to see where things start or how to handle place
names,
a lot is visible,
a lot is farm land,
a lot is mega-prisons plopped down on wide stretches of earth,
a lot is golden hills

but the hemisphere was not restricted although the state looks like it

and Samuel Johnson wrote the dictionary and beheld Scotland
from his own point of view, but not strictly from it

which means that the most basic reasons for going to Mexico persist

within the exchange

it should be epiphanic

I'm hard put to introduce myself

my skin was a talking skin and I was part of the conversing world

after the lucha libre we went to las cinco letras which stands for h o t e l
but can also stand for
m u s e o
or m e t r o—so you have to be clear!

In the pictures we took he is wearing the mask and kissing a gringa (me)

The other gringa was jealous of the picture

Us all together in the park
tired after shopping

Wanting a panorama to get all local on us,

You can want and want

I want to give you
the bunkest explanation,
the dud speech

But I keep putting in

My good ear

I see myself

Explaining,

Most people don't want to have a nasal voice,
one that's high-pitched

I keep thinking about the greatest mystery.

He is going to make
                a t-shirt

that says on the front,
                                I HATE GRINGOS
and on the back,

                                I LOVE GRINGAS

Part 1.

It's residential where Rand meets Cheney.

There's a man building the fence for his own house.

His name's Sean. He's divorced, but it's unclear.

Only on the weekends, chalk drawings appear on his sidewalk
un-mysterious,
primitive in the actual sense.

If nothing's hired out,
I'm a kit 'n kaboodle.

Which really was a make-up container that we girl cousins fought over in
the 80s. But—now it seems like another kind
of promise, the brink of
making good

Part 2.

This is my heart stealing the Jacksonian dream—

My dream was a hole through which to watch myself shower. I was using a new line of shampoo and conditioning products. The Woods line includes Cherry, Maple, Mahogany, and Cedar. The brunette is made more brunette.

In a dream I had blunt purchasing power,
I drilled the damn hole in the wall, I watched myself:

I was up and ahead, the one doing all the cajoling—the item flung down, the card whipped out—I was looking at everything the right amount of time, considering, moving on.

Tim the Tool Man Taylor, the selling point was incompetence, the laugh track attuned to the comic failure, the red flannels, home ownership, the right to screw up within one's provenance.

During the 90s the Herbal Essences line was a synonym for orgasm. There was this whole idea about the "I have to wash my hair" excuse. Everyone was excited about it in different ways.

Oh innuendo, get off of me. Go build something with the color of your hair

Part 3.

Betty the innkeeper floated right past the image
        of her fuckable self

It was never about that, it was inextricable

It's the hostess in the village
who knows the regulars

They touch her at the door
she's on
the way out

There was a tremble, a moment in which Tracy—the old maître d', the cougar—
got furious. She grabbed the new hostess. The inept hostess. The young hostess.
She said,
Don't ever let anyone push you around, you *run* this floor
Do you hear?

He was in the mafia and I was his goomah, but really he was queer and the guy
who fixed the computer shut the door behind him coyly,
but it was only me in the office, all ass & titties, all camel toe & whale tail, when
attempting to restock the wine, two bottles shattered, I ran to the kitchen
and said, *el vino se cayó, es mi culpa, lo siento,* but who gave a fuck that it was my
fault? Fault was a weak bastard, disinherited, unable to determine clean up duty,
unable to give me my true lot in life.
I'm floating free all pussy, all smiles

He said, smile like *that*
& you can break whatever you want

Somehow I kept splintering off into other women, I had no services to offer, I
mainly just hung out and chatted with people

Part 4.

In 4th grade we simulated
Inuit life—

In a fantasy I was hard theory, truth-value talking big. I was neutral in the
morning and neutral in the evening. Impartial: really, it's none of *my* business.
Nobody needs to know what I'm doing. I am unencumbered. Fishing
somewhere. Watching the animals. Setting up camp. Glowing favored in the
tavern, the mead hall, the annals.

In a nightmare I was an ethnographer at heart. I was saying nothing. I was a
wordy girl.

ABOUT THE AUTHOR

Rebecca Gaydos was born in Santa Barbara, California, where her mother and father worked as professional ballet dancers. At the University of California, Berkeley, she won the Eisner Prize in Poetry and earned her Ph.D. in English. She has taught literature and writing at Diablo Valley College, San Quentin State Prison, and the University of California, Berkeley.

GÜERA
by Rebecca Gaydos

Cover art © JW Collinge, courtesy of Santa Barbara Vintage Photos

Cover and interior text set in Optima LT Std and Minion Pro

Cover and interior design by Gillian Olivia Blythe Hamel

Offset printed in the United States
by Edwards Brothers Malloy, Ann Arbor, Michigan
On 55# Glatfelter B18 Antique
Acid Free Archival Quality Recycled Paper

Publication of this book was made possible in part by gifts from:
The New Place Fund
Robin & Curt Caton

Omnidawn Publishing
Oakland, California
2016

Rusty Morrison & Ken Keegan, senior editors & co-publishers
Gillian Olivia Blythe Hamel, managing editor
Cassandra Smith, poetry editor & book designer
Peter Burghardt, poetry editor
Sharon Zetter, poetry editor, book designer & development officer
Liza Flum, poetry editor & marketing assistant
Juliana Paslay, fiction editor
Gail Aronson, fiction editor
Kevin Peters, marketing assistant & OmniVerse Lit Scene editor
Cameron Stuart, marketing assistant
Sara Burant, administrative assistant
Avren Keating, administrative assistant
Josie Gallup, publicity assistant
SD Sumner, copyeditor